SOMALIA 2016 HUMAN RIGHTS REPORT

EXECUTIVE SUMMARY

The Federal Government of Somalia (FGS), formed in 2012, was led by President Hassan Sheikh Mohamud. Clan elders nominated the members of the House of the People of the Federal Parliament in 2012, and parliament elected Hassan Sheikh Mohamud as president later that year. Former Transitional Federal Government (TFG) president and presidential candidate, Sheikh Sharif, described the presidential vote as fair and conceded defeat. Indirect elections for the lower house of parliament, the new upper house, and the president, scheduled for August and September, had not been completed by year's end. The government of the self-declared Republic of Somaliland in the northwest and the regional government of Puntland in the northeast controlled their respective jurisdictions. The Interim Galmudug Administration (IGA), Interim Juba Administration (IJA), and Interim South West Administration (ISWA) did not fully control their jurisdictions. The terrorist organization al-Shabaab retained control of the Juba River Valley and maintained operational freedom of movement in many other areas in the south-central part of the country. Conflict during the year involving the government, militias, the African Union Mission in Somalia (AMISOM), and al-Shabaab resulted in death, injury, and displacement of civilians. AMISOM and Somali security forces did not conduct any major offensive operations to liberate additional areas during the year.

Civilian authorities did not maintain effective control over the security forces.

Major human rights abuses included killings of civilians by, Somali security forces, al-Shabaab, and unknown assailants. Violence and discrimination against women and girls, including rape and female genital mutilation/cutting (FGM/C), were widespread. Civilians did not have the ability to change their government through free and fair elections.

Other major human rights abuses included disappearances; torture and other cruel, inhuman, or degrading treatment or punishment; harsh prison conditions; arbitrary and politically motivated arrest and detention; denial of fair public trial; use of child soldiers; restrictions on freedoms of speech and press, assembly and association, religion, and movement; forced eviction and relocation of internally displaced persons (IDPs); disruption, diversion, and seizure of humanitarian assistance; corruption; trafficking in persons; abuse of and discrimination against minority clans and persons with disabilities; social stigmatization of lesbian, gay, bisexual, transgender, and intersex (LGBTI) individuals; restrictions on workers' rights and forced labor, including by children.

Impunity generally remained the norm. Government authorities took minimal steps to prosecute and punish officials who committed violations, particularly military and police officials accused of committing rape, killings, clan violence, and extortion of civilians.

Clan militias and al-Shabaab continued to commit grave abuses throughout the country, including extrajudicial and politically motivated killings; disappearances; cruel and unusual punishment; rape; and attacks on employees of nongovernmental organizations (NGOs), the United Nations, and diplomatic missions. It also blocked humanitarian assistance, conscripted child soldiers, and restricted freedoms of speech, press, assembly, and movement.

AMISOM troops killed civilians and committed sexual abuse and exploitation, including the rape of women and girls (see section 1.g.).

Section 1. Respect for the Integrity of the Person, Including Freedom from:

a. Arbitrary Deprivation of Life and other Unlawful or Politically Motivated Killings

Government security forces and allied militias, other persons wearing uniforms, regional security forces, al-Shabaab, and unknown assailants committed arbitrary or unlawful killings. Government and regional authorities executed persons without due process. Armed clashes and attacks killed civilians and aid workers (see section 1.g.). Impunity remained the norm.

Federal and regional forces killed protesters. For example, on March 26, police fired on civilians protesting the state formation process for Hiiraan and Middle Shabelle Regions in Beledweyne, killing one civilian and injuring four. In the Puntland-Somaliland contested regions of Sool and Sanaag, security forces used excessive force against residents who opposed Hargeisa-led voter registration efforts during the year. The use of force resulted in at least 10 deaths and multiple injuries.

On April 18, following days of clan clashes, a mother and her six children were killed when soldiers burned their house in a village near the town of Merka, Lower Shabelle Region.

In January 2015 government forces reportedly shot supporters of Ahlu Sunna Wal Jama (ASWJ), who were violently protesting against the federal government in Galhareeri, Galguduud Region; two persons died and others were injured. During the year the case was settled by local elders with assistance from FGS officials; no further details were available.

Military courts continued to try cases not legally within their jurisdiction and in proceedings that fell short of international standards. Federal and regional authorities sometimes executed those sentenced to death within days of the court's verdict, particularly in cases where defendants directly confessed their membership in al-Shabaab before the courts or in televised videos. National figures on executions were unreliable, but the UN Mission to Somalia (UNSOM) tracked 20 executions across the country during the year, including four of alleged members of al-Shabaab, 11 of armed forces members, and five of civilians. Human rights organizations questioned the military courts' ability to enforce appropriate safeguards with regard to due process, the right to seek pardon, or commutation of sentence as well as to implement sentences in a manner that meets international standards.

Fighting among clans and subclans, particularly over water and land resources, occurred throughout the year, particularly in Merka, Galkayo, and Hiiraan Regions (see section 6). Revenge killings occurred.

Al-Shabaab continued to kill civilians (see sections 1.g. and 6). The killings included al-Shabaab's execution of persons it accused of spying for and collaborating with the FGS, Somali national forces, and affiliated militias.

Al-Shabaab also reportedly killed journalists. For example, on June 5, gunmen suspected of belonging to al-Shabaab shot and killed a female journalist working for state-run station Radio Mogadishu.

Unidentified gunmen also killed persons with impunity, including members of parliament, judges, National Intelligence and Security Agency (NISA) agents, Somali National Army (SNA) soldiers, and other government officials, as well as journalists, traditional elders, and international organization workers.

On June 8, in Galkayo town, unidentified gunmen shot and killed Dhudi Yusuf Adan, a regional peace activist and head of the Mudug Women's Association. Al-Shabaab claimed responsibility. No investigation was conducted.

In a separate incident on September 27, unknown gunmen in Mogadishu killed Abdiaziz Mohamed Ali, a journalist with Radio Shabelle.

b. Disappearance

There were no reports that government authorities committed politically motivated or other disappearances. Al-Shabaab continued to abduct persons, including humanitarian workers. Pirates continued to hold persons kidnapped in previous years.

The 14 Iranian fishermen kidnapped in 2015 by al-Shabaab in Somali waters near El-Dheer, Galguduud Region, were released during the year.

Unlike in previous years, there were no reports of piracy. The vessel and crew of a Pakistani-owned, Iranian-flagged vessel hijacked by armed men in November 2015 were released during the year. On October 23, the 26 crewmembers of the *Naham 3*, captured in 2012, were released.

c. Torture and Other Cruel, Inhuman, or Degrading Treatment or Punishment

The provisional federal constitution prohibits torture and inhuman treatment. Nevertheless, torture and other cruel, inhuman, or degrading treatment or punishment occurred. The UN Monitoring Group on Somalia and Eritrea (SEMG) reported it received allegations that NISA officials committed torture. Government forces, allied militia, other men wearing uniforms, and AMISOM troops committed sexual violence, including rape (see section 1.g.).

Federal and regional authorities used excessive force against journalists, demonstrators, and detainees, which resulted in deaths and injuries.

NISA agents routinely conducted mass security sweeps despite having no legal mandate to arrest or detain. NISA held detainees for prolonged periods without following due process and mistreated suspects during interrogations.

Al-Shabaab imposed harsh punishment on persons in areas under its control (see sections 1.a. and 1.g.).

Clan violence sometimes resulted in civilian deaths and injuries (see sections 1.g.

and 6).

Prison and Detention Center Conditions

Prison conditions in most areas of the country remained harsh due to poor sanitation and hygiene, inadequate food and water, and lack of medical care. Conditions were better in Central Mogadishu Prison, but overcrowding was a problem. Two new facilities--Garowe Prison in Puntland (completed in 2014) and Hargeisa Prison in Somaliland (completed in 2011)--met international standards and reportedly were well managed. Prisons in territory controlled by al-Shabaab and in remote areas where traditional authorities controlled holding areas were generally inaccessible to international observers. Prison conditions in such areas were believed to be harsh and at times life threatening.

Physical Conditions: Overcrowding in urban prisons--particularly following large security incidents involving arrests--sometimes occurred. Authorities sometimes held juveniles and adults, due in part to the belief that juveniles were safer when housed with members of their own subclan. Prison authorities often did not separate pretrial detainees from convicted prisoners, particularly in the southern and central regions.

Only inmates in Central Mogadishu Prison, Garowe Prison, and Hargeisa Prison had daily access to showers, sanitary facilities, adequate food and water, and outdoor exercise. Authorities in some states, however, made modest improvements in these areas in recent years with support from international organizations. Inmates in most prisons relied on their family and clan to supplement food and water provisions. The incarceration of juveniles at the request of families who wanted their children disciplined remained a problem, primarily in Puntland and Somaliland. This practice occurred mainly with diaspora children, whose families paid prison authorities to hold children with substance abuse problems as a form of rehabilitation due to the lack of other treatment options.

Authorities generally required the families of inmates to pay the cost of health services; inmates without family or clan support had limited access to such services. Disease outbreaks, such as tuberculosis and cholera, continued to occur, particularly in overcrowded prisons, such as Mogadishu. Such outbreaks could be life threatening during the rainy season.

Prison infrastructure often was dilapidated, and untrained guards were unable to provide security.

Information on deaths rates in prisons and pretrial detention centers was unavailable.

Al-Shabaab detained persons in areas under its control in the southern and central regions. Those detained were incarcerated under inhuman conditions for relatively minor "offenses," such as smoking, having illicit content on cell phones, listening to music, watching or playing soccer, wearing a brassiere, or not wearing a hijab.

Administration: Apart from Central Mogadishu, Garowe, and Hargeisa Prisons, which tracked prisoners and their status, recordkeeping generally was inadequate. Most prisons did not have ombudsmen.

Federal law does not specifically allow prisoners to submit complaints to judicial authorities without censorship. Somaliland law, however, allows prisoners to submit complaints to judicial authorities without censorship, and prisoners reportedly submitted such complaints.

Prisoners in Central Mogadishu, Garowe, and Hargeisa Prisons had adequate access to visitors and religious observance; infrastructure limitations in other prisons throughout the country impeded such activities. Many prisoners relied on visitors to provide supplemental food and water.

Independent Monitoring: Somaliland authorities and government authorities in Puntland and Mogadishu permitted prison monitoring by independent nongovernmental observers during the year. Representatives from the UN Office on Drugs and Crime visited prisons in Bosaso, Garowe, and Hargeisa several times. UNSOM representatives, other UN organizations, and humanitarian institutions visited a few prisons throughout the country. Geographic inaccessibility and insecurity impeded such monitoring in territory controlled by al-Shabaab or in remote areas where traditional authorities controlled holding areas.

Improvements: Building on improvements at Central Mogadishu Prison that started with the 2015 appointment of a new federal custodial corps commissioner, authorities relocated juvenile, nonviolent, and female prisoners to a renovated wing of the prison with less overcrowding and better access to running water, toilets, and modest educational and vocational programs. Independent monitors visited Central Mogadishu, Garowe, and Hargeisa Prisons and confirmed improved access and conditions.

d. Arbitrary Arrest or Detention

Although the provisional federal constitution prohibits illegal detention, government security forces and allied militias, regional authorities, clan militias, and al-Shabaab arbitrarily arrested and detained persons (see section 1.g.).

Role of the Police and Security Apparatus

The provisional federal constitution states that the armed forces are responsible for assuring the country's sovereignty, independence, and territorial integrity and that the national federal and state police are responsible for protecting lives, property, peace, and security. Police were generally ineffective and lacked sufficient equipment and training. In Mogadishu, for example, police lacked sufficient vehicles to transfer prisoners from cells to courts or to medical facilities. There were reports of police engaging in corrupt practices.

AMISOM and the SNA worked to maintain order in areas of the southern and central regions. The FGS regularly relied on NISA forces to perform police work, often calling on them to arrest and detain civilians without warrants. Some towns and rural areas in the southern and central regions remained under the control of al-Shabaab and affiliated militias. The Ministry of Defense is responsible for controlling the armed forces. Police forces fall under a mix of local and regional administrations and the government. The national police force remained under the jurisdiction of the Ministry of Internal Security, while regional authorities maintained police forces under their areas' interior or security ministries.

Civilian authorities did not maintain effective control of security forces. Security forces abused civilians and often failed to prevent or respond to societal violence. Although authorities sometimes used military courts to try individuals believed to be responsible for abuse, they generally did not investigate abuse by police, army, or militia members; a culture of impunity was widespread. For example, on August 1, in Mogadishu an SNA soldier reportedly killed a bus driver during an extortion attempt. The soldier was not arrested.

The Ministry of Defense's control over the army remained tenuous but improved somewhat with the support of international partners. At year's end the army consisted of between 11,000 and 14,000 soldiers, according to estimates by international organizations. The bulk of forces were located in Middle Shabelle and Lower Shabelle regions, as well as in the ISWA and IJA. The Ministry of Defense exerted some control over forces in the greater Mogadishu area, extending as far south as Lower Shabelle Region, west to Baidoa, Bay Region, and north to Jowhar, Middle Shabelle Region. Army forces and progovernment militia sometimes operated alongside AMISOM in areas where AMISOM was deployed.

The federal police force maintained its presence in all 17 districts of the capital. AMISOM-formed police units complemented local and FGS policing efforts in Mogadishu. These police officers provided mentoring and advisory support on basic police duties, respect for human rights, crime prevention strategies, community policing, and search procedures. More than 300 AMISOM police officers worked alongside the formed units to provide training to national police.

Arrest Procedures and Treatment of Detainees

The provisional federal constitution provides for arrested persons to be brought before judicial authorities within 48 hours. The law requires warrants based on sufficient evidence and issued by authorized officials for the apprehension of suspects. The law also provides that arrestees receive prompt notification of the charges against them and judicial determinations, prompt access to a lawyer and family members, and other legal protections. Adherence to these safeguards was rare. The FGS made arrests without warrants and detained individuals arbitrarily. The government sometimes kept high-profile prisoners associated with al-Shabaab in safe houses before officially charging them. The law provides for bail, although authorities did not always respect this provision. Authorities rarely provided indigent persons a lawyer. The government held suspects under house arrest, particularly high-ranking defectors from al-Shabaab with strong clan connections. Security force members and corrupt judicial officers, politicians, and clan elders used their influence to have detainees released.

Arbitrary Arrest: Government and regional authorities arbitrarily arrested and detained numerous persons, including persons accused of terrorism and supporting al-Shabaab. Authorities frequently used allegations of al-Shabaab affiliation to justify arbitrary arrests (see section 1.a.).

Government, regional authorities, and clan militias arbitrarily arrested journalists.

Government forces conducted operations to arrest youths they perceived as suspicious without executing warrants.

<u>Pretrial Detention</u>: Lengthy pretrial detention was common, although estimates were unavailable on the average length of pretrial detention or the percentage of the prison population being held in pretrial detention. The large number of detainees, shortage of judges and court administrators, and judicial inefficiency resulted in trial delays.

<u>Detainee's Ability to Challenge Lawfulness of Detention before a Court</u>: The law provides detainees the right to challenge in court the legal basis of their detention, but only politicians and business persons could exercise this right effectively.

e. Denial of Fair Public Trial

The provisional federal constitution states, "The judiciary is independent of the legislative and executive branches of government." The civilian judicial system, however, remained largely nonfunctional across the country. Some regions established local courts that depended on the dominant local clan and associated factions for their authority. The judiciary in most areas relied on some combination of traditional and customary law, sharia, and formal law. The judiciary was subject to influence and corruption and was strongly influenced by clan-based politics. Authorities did not respect court orders. Civilian judges often feared trying cases, leaving military courts to try the majority of civilian cases.

In Somaliland, functional courts existed, although there was a serious shortage of trained judges, limited legal documentation upon which to build judicial precedent, and increasing allegations of corruption. Somaliland's hybrid judicial system incorporates sharia (Islamic law), customary law, and formal law, but they were not well integrated. There was widespread interference in the judicial process, and government officials regularly intervened to influence cases, particularly those involving journalists. International NGOs reported local officials interfered in legal matters and invoked the public order law to detain and incarcerate persons without trial.

Puntland courts, while functional, lacked the capacity to provide equal protection under the law and faced similar challenges and limitations as courts in Somaliland.

Traditional clan elders mediated conflicts throughout the country. Clans frequently used and applied traditional justice practices swiftly. Traditional judgments sometimes held entire clans or subclans responsible for alleged violations by individuals.

Trial Procedures

The provisional federal constitution states, "Every person has the right to a fair public hearing by an independent and impartial court or tribunal, to be held within a reasonable time." According to the provisional federal constitution, individuals have the right to a presumption of innocence. They also have the right to be informed promptly and in detail of the charges against them in a language they understand, although the constitution is unclear on whether the right to translation applies through all appeals. Detainees have the right to be brought before a competent court within 48 hours of arrest, to communicate with an attorney of their choice (or have one provided at public expense if indigent), and may not be compelled to incriminate themselves. The law extends these rights to all citizens, but authorities did not respect most rights relating to trial procedures. The provisional constitution does not address access to government-held evidence, confronting witnesses, the right to appeal a court's ruling, the provision of sufficient time and facilities to prepare a defense, or the right to present one's own evidence and witnesses.

Military courts tried civilians. Defendants in military courts rarely had legal representation or the right to appeal. Authorities sometimes executed those sentenced to death within days of the court's verdict (see section 1.a.). Some government officials continued to claim that a 2011 state of emergency decree gave military courts jurisdiction over crimes, including those committed by civilians, in parts of Mogadishu from which al-Shabaab had retreated. There was no clear government policy indicating whether this decree remained in effect.

In Somaliland, defendants generally enjoyed a presumption of innocence and the right to a public trial, to be present at trial, and to consult an attorney at all stages of criminal proceedings. The government did not always inform defendants promptly and in detail of the charges against them and did not always provide access to government-held evidence. The government did not provide defendants with dedicated facilities to prepare a defense but generally provided adequate time to prepare. The government provided defendants with free interpretation or paid for private interpretation if they declined government-offered interpretation from the moment charged through all appeals. Defendants could question witnesses, present witnesses and evidence in their defense, and appeal court verdicts.

Somaliland provided free legal representation for defendants who faced serious criminal charges and could not afford a private attorney. Defendants had the right not to be compelled to testify or confess guilt. A functioning legal aid clinic existed.

In Puntland clan elders resolved the majority of cases using customary law. The administration's more formalized judicial system addressed cases of those with no clan representation. Defendants generally enjoyed a presumption of innocence, the right to a public trial, the right to be present and consult an attorney at all stages of criminal proceedings, and the right to appeal. Authorities did not always inform defendants promptly and in detail of the charges against them and did not always provide access to government-held evidence. Defendants had the right to present their own witnesses and evidence. Authorities did not provide defendants with dedicated facilities to prepare a defense but generally provided adequate time to prepare. Puntland authorities provided defendants with free interpretation services when needed. The government often delayed court proceedings for an unreasonable period.

There was no functioning formal judicial system in al-Shabaab-controlled areas. In sharia courts defendants generally did not defend themselves, present witnesses, or have an attorney represent them.

Political Prisoners and Detainees

The number of persons detained during the year for politically motivated reasons was unknown. Government and regional authorities arrested journalists as well as other persons critical of authorities.

Somaliland authorities continued to detain Somaliland residents employed by the federal government in Mogadishu, sometimes for extended periods. Somaliland authorities did not authorize officials in Mogadishu to represent Somaliland within or to the federal Somali government and viewed such actions as treason, punishable under the constitution of Somaliland.

During the year Ahmed Hussein Sitin, a member of the federal parliament arrested and detained in July 2015 for returning to Somaliland without government authorization, was released.

Civil Judicial Procedures and Remedies

There were no known lawsuits seeking damages for, or cessation of, human rights violations in any region during the year, although the provisional federal constitution provides for "adequate procedures for redress of violations of human rights."

Property Restitution

In Mogadishu the government and others evicted persons, primarily IDP returnees, from their homes without due process (see section 2.d.).

f. Arbitrary or Unlawful Interference with Privacy, Family, Home, or Correspondence

According to the provisional federal constitution, "every person has the right to own, use, enjoy, sell, and transfer property" and the private home is inviolable. Nonetheless, authorities searched property without warrants.

During the year AMISOM and Somali forces retained control over several areas liberated from al-Shabaab in 2015. The return of IDPs to areas recently liberated continued to result in disputes over land ownership. There was no formal mechanism to address such disputes.

Government and regional authorities harassed relatives of al-Shabaab members.

g. Abuses in Internal Conflicts

Killings: Conflict during the year involving the government, militias, AMISOM, and al-Shabaab resulted in death, injury, and displacement of civilians. Clan-based political violence involved revenge killings and attacks on civilian settlements. Clashes between clan-based forces and with al-Shabaab in the Galmudug, Lower Shabelle, and Hiiraan Regions, also resulted in deaths.

Somaliland used military force to suppress opponents of voter registration in contested regions (see section 1.a.).

According to UNSOM reports, security force attacks against al-Shabaab, other armed groups or individuals, and civilians between January and August resulted in 492 civilian deaths, with casualties attributed to the SNA (44 deaths, 76 injured), AMISOM (eight deaths, nine injured), and Kenya Defense Forces operating bilaterally (38 deaths, including four children, and 11 injured). Al-Shabaab caused significant civilian casualties, including 214 deaths and 346 injured, during that period.

Al-Shabaab committed politically motivated killings that targeted civilians affiliated with the government and attacks on humanitarian NGO employees, UN staff, and diplomatic missions. Al-Shabaab often used suicide attacks, mortar attacks, and improvised explosive devices (IEDs). It also killed prominent peace activists, community leaders, clan elders, and their family members for their roles in peace building, and it beheaded persons accused of spying for and collaborating with Somali national forces and affiliated militias.

On August 21, al-Shabaab used vehicle-borne IEDs to attack a government office located next to a market in Galkayo; 23 persons were killed, including government officials, security personnel, students, and merchants.

Abductions: From January to September, al-Shabaab abducted 152 persons, 80 of whom it subsequently released.

Following a September 22 attack on a Kenyan police station in the border town of Liboi, al-Shabaab publicly claimed it had captured two Kenyan police officers. According to Kenyan officials, the two officers remained missing at year's end.

Physical Abuse, Punishment, and Torture: Government forces, allied militias, men wearing uniforms, and AMISOM troops used excessive force, including torture, and raped women and girls, including IDPs. While the army arrested some security force members accused of such abuse, impunity was the norm.

Al-Shabaab also committed sexual violence, including through forced marriages.

On May 7, 14 AMISOM soldiers from Ethiopia allegedly raped two girls, ages 15 and 17, in the Galguduug Region. AMISOM investigated but stated it could not corroborate the facts sufficiently to convene a board of inquiry.

According to UN Mine Action Service, IEDs killed 267 persons and injured 727; land mines killed one person and injured another; explosive remnants of war killed one person and injured 13.

Child Soldiers: During the year there were continued reports of the SNA and allied militia, the ASWJ, and al-Shabaab using child soldiers.

UN officials documented the recruitment and use during the year of 1,744 children (1,679 boys, 65 girls), including by al-Shabaab (1,091), the SNA (169), clan militia (415), the ASWJ (67), and other armed elements (two). There were 1,381 children

(1,306 boys, 75 girls) abducted: 857 by al-Shabaab, 373 by the SNA, 125 by clan militia, and 12 by the ASWJ, with AMISOM and unknown armed elements responsible for seven abductions each. More than half of the children al-Shabaab abducted were used to increase its numbers before joint SNA/AMISOM operations, including the March attack in Puntland. The number recruited during the first half of the year equaled the total number recruited throughout 2015, demonstrating an increase in al-Shabaab recruitment. Children abducted by AMISOM were typically released unharmed within a couple of days. The reason for the abductions remained unclear.

Implementation of the government's 2012 action plan with the United Nations to end the recruitment and use of children by the national army remained incomplete.

The SNA's Child Protection Unit (CPU) reported it conducted training awareness campaigns in Mogadishu, Guul Wadayasha, and at the Siyad Army Base on the importance of preventing child recruitment into the security forces. The CPU and regional focal points continued to monitor the SNA, including conducting inspections of the main SNA training center in Mogadishu and several subnational military recruitment and stipend payment locations in Mogadishu, Guul Wadayasha, and at the Siyad Army base. The CPU did not identify any child soldiers during the year.

During the year the United Nations supported the reintegration of 854 children associated with armed forces (722 boys, 132 girls) into their families and communities. Reintegration activities included the provision of psychosocial assistance, "back-to-school" support programs, and vocational training.

Due to the absence of birth registration systems, it was often difficult to determine the age of national security force recruits.

Al-Shabaab continued to recruit and force children to participate in direct hostilities, including suicide attacks. Al-Shabaab raided schools, madrassas, and mosques to recruit children. Children in al-Shabaab training camps were subjected to grueling physical training, inadequate diet, weapons training, physical punishment, and religious training. The training also included forcing children to punish and execute other children. Al-Shabaab used children in combat, including placing them in front of other fighters to serve as human shields and suicide bombers. In addition, al-Shabaab used children in support roles, such as carrying ammunition, water, and food; removing injured and dead militants; gathering intelligence; and serving as guards. The organization sometimes used children to plant roadside bombs and other explosive devices. The Somali press frequently carried accounts of al-Shabaab indoctrinating children at schools and forcibly recruiting students into its ranks.

Authorities transferred children separated from armed groups to the UN Children's Fund (UNICEF).

In March government forces in Puntland and Galkayo captured 108 children fighting alongside al-Shabaab in Puntland and Galkayo. Of the 108 children in Puntland, soldiers transferred 70 to Mogadishu to receive reintegration support from an NGO supported by UNICEF. Although the president of Puntland expressed his commitment not to execute any of the 108 children, 10 received death sentences and 28 received prison sentences ranging from 10 to 20 years, based on age. UNICEF continued to advocate for the reduction of sentences and for the transfer of the remaining 38 children for integration support.

<u>Other Conflict-related Abuse</u>: Armed groups, particularly al-Shabaab but also government forces and militia, deliberately restricted the passage of relief supplies and other items indispensable to the survival of the civilian population as well as access by humanitarian organizations, particularly in the southern and central regions.

Humanitarian workers regularly faced checkpoints, roadblocks, extortion, car-jacking, and bureaucratic obstacles. Humanitarian organizations were often treated with suspicion and extorted. In the first six months of the year, according to the United Nations, more than 80 security-related incidents with direct effect on humanitarian organizations occurred, including the deaths of five aid workers, injuring of eight, arrest of 10, abduction of three, and physical assault on five.

Government forces seized relief supplies. For example, on March 31, SNA forces reportedly intercepted a World Food Program (WFP) truck traveling from Mombasa, Kenya, to El Wak, Somalia, and stole the food. The El Wak local administration recovered the consignment. In May and June, government authorities seized WFP food at the Mogadishu airport following anonymous and incorrect reports that it had expired. While in government custody, the condition of the seized food deteriorated and it was no longer fit for human consumption.

Al-Shabaab also seized relief supplies. For example, on April 13, al-Shabaab seized a truck transporting WFP food commodities near El Wak. WFP halted critical activities outside El Wak, including the treatment of acute malnutrition, until the driver, truck, and commodities were released.

Conflict in contested territories of Sool and Sanaag, between Somaliland and Puntland, restricted humanitarian access. NGOs reported incidents of harassment by local authorities in both Somaliland and Puntland.

Al-Shabaab blocked humanitarian access to 28 districts in southern and central Somalia, including critical transportation routes to areas liberated by AMISOM. Human Rights Watch reported al-Shabaab imposed blockades around Hudur, Bulo-Burte, Elbur, Qoryoley, and other towns that had been liberated by AMISOM and Somali government forces, severely restricting the movement of goods, assistance, and persons.

Al-Shabaab restricted medical care, including by impeding civilian travel to other areas to receive care, destroying medications provided by humanitarian agencies, and closing medical clinics.

International aid organizations evacuated their staff or halted food distribution and other aid-related activities in al-Shabaab-controlled areas due to killings, extortion, threats, harassment, expulsions, and prohibitions by al-Shabaab. On March 15, for example, unidentified gunmen kidnapped three aid workers in the southwest. International aid agencies continued to rely on Somali staff and local organizations to deliver relief assistance, particularly in remote rural areas.

Because of fighting between al-Shabaab, AMISOM, and the SNA, al-Shabaab's humanitarian access restrictions and taxation on livestock, and the lack of security, many residents in al-Shabaab-controlled areas fled to refugee camps in Kenya and Ethiopia and IDP camps in other areas of the country. ASWJ militias and federal forces skirmished throughout the year, displacing civilian populations.

Section 2. Respect for Civil Liberties, Including:

a. Freedom of Speech and Press

The provisional federal constitution provides for freedom of speech and press, but neither federal nor regional authorities respected these rights. The government, government-aligned militias, authorities in Somaliland and Puntland, ISWA, IGA, IJA, ASWJ, al-Shabaab, and unknown assailants killed, abused, and harassed journalists with impunity (see sections 1.a. and 1.g.).

The Somaliland constitution prohibits publication or circulation of exaggerated or tendentious news capable of disturbing public order, and officials used the provision to charge and arrest journalists.

The Puntland constitution limits freedom of opinion and expression through broadly worded limitations--including conformity with moral dignity, national stability, and personal rights of others--and allows for exceptions from the right to freedom of expression in times of war or other public emergency.

<u>Freedom of Speech and Expression</u>: Individuals in government-controlled areas risked reprisal for criticizing government officials, particularly for alleged official corruption or suggestions that officials were unable to manage security matters.

<u>Press and Media Freedoms</u>: Print media consisted largely of short, photocopied independent daily newspapers, many of which the government owned, that were published in the larger cities. Several of these publications included criticism of political leaders and other prominent persons.

Citizens obtained news from foreign and domestic radio and television broadcasts. According to the African Union, approximately 50 radio stations operated throughout the southern and central regions as did one shortwave station in Mogadishu. As in previous years, Somaliland authorities continued to prohibit the establishment of independent FM stations, although several independent newspapers existed. All FM stations in Somaliland were government owned. There were at least six independent radio stations in Puntland.

Government and regional authorities temporarily closed media outlets, citing as reasons defamation or offending the president and other national leaders.

Somaliland authorities continued to fine and arbitrarily arrest journalists for defamation and other alleged crimes, including meeting with colleagues. Between April and August, Somaliland authorities arrested nine journalists, including one who worked with the state-owned television station, for attempting to meet in private with a member of the opposition party. Prison terms ranged from a few days to several months, and fines could be as high as 573,000 shillings ($1,000).

On June 23, Puntland police, on orders of Puntland's minister of information, closed Radio Daljir offices for one week following the station's interview with Abdisalan Gallan, former governor of Bari Region, who was fired for opposing the administration. Local media reported that the minister, Mohamoud Hassan

So'adde, called the station following the interview and threatened violent reprisal for interviewing Gallan.

<u>Violence and Harassment</u>: The government executed a journalist during the year (see section 1.a.).

NISA arrested 16 journalists in Mogadishu, Beledweyne, Jowhar, and Kismayo during the year. Most were released without charge or after paying a fine.

According to the Somaliland Journalists Association, local authorities continued to harass and arbitrarily detain journalists systematically. In May, Somaliland police, at the behest of the mayor of Berbera, arrested several journalists, including Abdirashid Abdiwahaab Ibraahim, chairman of the independent newspaper *Foor*. The government accused the journalists of reporting on a member of the Berbera local government council who expressed skepticism about an agreement between the Somaliland government and Dubai Ports World on management of the Berbera port and for alleging that the president's family received significant kickbacks from the agreement.

Journalists based in the Lower Juba Region continued to report that local security authorities harassed them.

On August 20, police arrested Somaliland journalist Saed Mohamoud Gahayr for publishing articles and social media posts that criticized Somaliland authorities. On October 15, the Hargeisa Regional Court acquitted Gahayr, as it lacked sufficient evidence. The prosecutor filed an urgent appeal, and the journalist remained in detention at year's end.

Al-Shabaab and unknown gunmen killed five journalists and harassed and threatened others. Journalists reported al-Shabaab threatened to kill them if they did not report positively on antigovernment attacks.

<u>Censorship or Content Restrictions</u>: Journalists engaged in rigorous self-censorship to avoid reprisals.

On August 30, the governor of Hiiraan Region, Yusuf Ahmed Hagar, warned journalists in Beledweyne against reporting on the activities of politicians whose campaigns were not "authorized" by the government and threatened consequences for those who failed to comply.

Al-Shabaab banned journalists from reporting news that undermined Islamic law as interpreted by al-Shabaab and forbade persons in areas under its control from listening to international media outlets.

Libel/Slander Laws: Puntland and Somaliland authorities prosecuted journalists for libel. For example, in May the Somaliland security service arrested Mohamed Mohamud Yusuf and Abdirashid Abdiwahab Ibrahim--the editor and journalist, respectively, of an independent newspaper--for a report that criticized the government. The attorney general pressed criminal charges, including publication of "false news" and "defaming and smearing the president and first lady of Somaliland." Both men were released on bail in June.

National Security: Federal and regional authorities cited national security concerns to suppress criticism and prevent press coverage of opposition political figures. For example, on September 22, airport security officials released a statement banning media representatives from entering the airport for 60 days, reportedly due to security concerns during the electoral period.

Internet Freedom

Authorities restricted access to the internet, but there were no credible reports that the government monitored private online communications without appropriate legal authority.

Al-Shabaab prohibited companies from providing access to the internet and forced telecommunication companies to shut data services in al-Shabaab-controlled areas.

UNSOM reported that internet service providers (ISPs) in February blocked 29 of 35 sites in compliance with a November 2015 order from the attorney general requiring the Ministry of Post and Telecommunications to block 35 websites considered a threat to national security due to their criticism of the government. Of the 35 sites identified, ISPs refused to block the six websites with links to al-Shabaab on the basis that the government was unable to protect them from retaliation.

According to the International Telecommunication Union, less than 2 percent of the population used the internet in 2015.

Academic Freedom and Cultural Events

Academics practiced self-censorship.

The Puntland administration required individuals to obtain government permits to conduct academic research.

Except in al-Shabaab-controlled areas, there were no official restrictions on attending cultural events, playing music, or going to the cinema. The security situation, however, effectively restricted access to and organization of cultural events in the southern and central regions.

b. Freedom of Peaceful Assembly and Association

Freedom of Assembly

The federal provisional constitution provides for freedom of assembly, but the government limited this right. A general lack of security effectively limited this right as well. Federal and regional authorities killed protesters (see section 1.a.). The federal Ministry of Internal Security continued to require its approval for all public gatherings, citing security concerns, such as the risk of attack by al-Shabaab suicide bombers. Suppression of opposition meetings and gatherings increased during the election cycle, which began in August and continued at year's end.

On July 9, the minister of internal security released a letter banning all meetings in Mogadishu hotels without prior approval from the ministry. On September 19, Mogadishu mayor Yusuf Hassan Jimale stated that opposition demonstrations would not be allowed in the capital due to security concerns; authorities did not impose any such restrictions on progovernment demonstrations.

The Somaliland government banned opposition political rallies outside the official campaign window, which typically began 45 days ahead of a scheduled national election. Authorities did not impose any such restrictions on progovernment rallies. On July 25, according to the Somaliland Journalists Association, Somaliland's minister of national planning suspended three workshops for journalists in reprisal for media accusations that he mismanaged the Somaliland Development Fund.

Al-Shabaab did not allow any gatherings without its prior consent.

Freedom of Association

The provisional federal constitution provides for freedom of association, but government officials harassed NGO workers. There were also reports that regional authorities restricted freedom of association. Al-Shabaab did not allow most international NGOs to operate.

Persons in the southern and central regions outside of al-Shabaab-controlled areas could freely join civil society organizations focusing on a wide range of problems. Citizens generally respected civil society organizations for their ability to deliver social services in the absence of functioning government ministries.

Regional administrations took steps to control or gain benefit from humanitarian organizations, including by imposing duplicative registration requirements at different levels of government; attempting to control humanitarian organization contracting, procurement, and staffing; and opaque and vague taxation.

Some Puntland civil society members alleged interference by security forces in political activities during the year. For example, in July authorities arrested and detained Yacub Mohamed Abdalla, a former minister and director of a local NGO, for publicly criticizing the Puntland president's record on development.

c. Freedom of Religion

See the Department of State's *International Religious Freedom Report* at www.state.gov/religiousfreedomreport/.

d. Freedom of Movement, Internally Displaced Persons, Protection of Refugees, and Stateless Persons

The provisional federal constitution states that all persons lawfully residing in the country have the right to freedom of movement, to choose their residence, and to leave the country. Freedom of movement, however, was restricted in some areas.

Abuse of Migrants, Refugees, and Stateless Persons: Refugees lacked access to protection through law enforcement and the justice system. Refugees reported incidents of extortion, robbery, and sexual violence to the Office of the UN High Commissioner for Refugees (UNHCR).

The government and Somaliland authorities cooperated with UNHCR and the International Organization for Migration (IOM) to assist IDPs, refugees, returning refugees, asylum seekers, stateless persons, and other persons of concern.

During the year dialogue continued between humanitarian agencies, the FGS, and regional authorities to remove checkpoints and facilitate movement of humanitarian assistance, food aid, and essential commodities.

<u>In-country Movement</u>: Checkpoints operated by government forces, allied groups, armed militias, clan factions, and al-Shabaab inhibited movement and exposed citizens to looting, extortion, harassment, and violence. Roadblocks manned by armed actors and attacks on humanitarian personnel severely restricted movement and the delivery of aid in southern and central sectors of the country.

Al-Shabaab and other nonstate armed actors continued to ban commercial activities in the areas they controlled in the Bakool, Bay, Gedo, and Hiraan Regions and impeded the delivery of humanitarian assistance. For example, on June 19, armed men attacked and looted a truck convoy contracted by a humanitarian agency to deliver food aid and supplies in the Bakool Region and destroyed the vehicles.

Attacks against humanitarian workers and assets impeded the delivery of aid to vulnerable populations. During the first seven months of the year, there were more than 90 violent incidents targeting humanitarian agencies, as a result of which seven humanitarian workers were killed and eight injured, 10 were arrested, three abducted, and five assaulted while in detention. On July 26, a UNHCR staff member, 13 UNHCR employees, and 11 security personnel were killed during an al-Shabaab attack on the UNHCR compound in Mogadishu.

Somaliland prohibited federal officials, including those of Somaliland origin who purported to represent Hargeisa's interests in Mogadishu, from entering Somaliland. It also prevented its citizens from traveling to Mogadishu to participate in FGS processes or in cultural activities.

IGA officials denied entry to Puntland residents and continued to arrest drivers with Puntland license plates. The practice began in January 2015, when the former Galmudug traffic supervisor announced that drivers of vehicles with Puntland plates would be fined, arrested, and detained for 24 hours.

Puntland authorities continued to ban the transport of goods by road from the port of Berbera in Somaliland to towns in Puntland, including Garowe and Galkayo. The ban limited the ability of aid workers to deliver humanitarian supplies, such as food, livestock vaccination equipment, nutritional supplements, and education materials, to vulnerable populations in Puntland.

Foreign Travel: Few citizens had the means to obtain passports. In view of
widespread passport fraud, many foreign governments did not recognize Somali
passports as valid travel documents.

Internally Displaced Persons

Conflict, including fighting between clan militias in the Lower Shabelle,
Galmudug, and Hiraan regions, and drought resulted in more than 1.1 million
IDPs, primarily in the southern and central regions; nearly 400,000 IDPs were
located in Mogadishu.

Forced deportations from Saudi Arabia continued during the year; approximately
85,000 Somalis have been forcibly repatriated from Saudi Arabia since 2013.
Many returnees were unable to return to their places of origin and became IDPs.

Somalis and citizens from other countries fleeing the conflict in Yemen sought
refuge in Somalia. While flows from Yemen have declined since August 2015,
more than 33,500 individuals have fled to Somalia since March 2015. This
included more than 28,800 Somali nationals, 4,500 Yemeni refugees, and
approximately 300 migrants of other nationalities. UNHCR protected IDPs and
provided them with temporary lodging and financial assistance. Since March 2015
the IOM has assisted more than 10,500 arrivals with onward transportation to their
final destinations; the majority traveled to Mogadishu.

Government and regional authorities provided negligible protection and assistance
to IDPs and sometimes actively participated in their displacement. Private persons
with claims to land and government authorities, for example, regularly pursued the
forceful eviction of IDPs in Mogadishu. Some IDPs and humanitarian agencies
criticized local authorities for tacitly endorsing the forceful relocation of IDPs to
insecure areas in Mogadishu. Somali authorities did not prevent the forced
displacement of persons from shelters to camps on the outskirts of the city.

From January to August, authorities forcibly evicted approximately 91,000
persons, mostly IDPs; more than 78,000 were relocated to the south central part of
the country, primarily Mogadishu. Insecure land tenure and limited land title
verification contributed to the scale of forced evictions.

An April 2015 a Human Rights Watch report alleged that Somali national police,

NISA forces, and city council police forcibly evicted an estimated 21,000 displaced persons in Mogadishu during March. The report claimed Somali authorities beat some of those evicted, destroyed their shelters, and left them without water, food, or other assistance. According to the report, authorities failed to provide adequate notification and compensation to the communities facing eviction and did not provide viable relocation or local integration options as required by international law. The report claimed that none of the evicted persons interviewed for the report had seen an official written eviction order, and most were unaware of the planned evictions.

Government forces and aligned militia looted and collaborated in the diversion of humanitarian aid from intended beneficiaries in Mogadishu. Most international aid organizations previously evacuated their staff or halted food distribution and other aid-related activities in al-Shabaab-controlled areas due to continued killings, extortion, threats, and harassment.

Government forces, allied militias, men wearing uniforms, and AMISOM troops committed sexual violence, including rape of IDPs in and around Mogadishu. Many of the victims were children. Women and children living in IDP settlements were particularly vulnerable to rape by armed men, including government soldiers and militia members. Gatekeepers in control of some IDP camps reportedly forced girls and women to provide sex in exchange for food and services within the camps.

Protection of Refugees

Access to Asylum: The provisional federal constitution states that every person who has sought refuge in the country has the right not to be returned or taken to any country in which that person has a well-founded fear of persecution. There was no official system for providing such protection.

Somaliland continued to register asylum seekers with the assistance of UNHCR. The Somaliland Ministry of Rehabilitation, Resettlement, and Reconstruction had only limited resources and registered fewer than 1,000 new arrivals and asylum seekers during the year. In some instances the Somaliland government refused to register Ethiopians and Eritreans as asylum seekers. Some Yemenis with Somali origins were classified as returnees instead of refugees, shifting the costs associated with resettlement from UNHCR to the government of Somaliland.

Employment: Employment opportunities were limited for refugees, Somali returnees, and other vulnerable populations. Refugee returnees from Kenya reported limited employment opportunities in areas of return in the southern and central sections of the country.

Access to Basic Services: The FGS continued to work with the international community to improve access to basic services, employment, and durable solutions for displaced populations.

On August 29, the IJA began blocking all voluntary refugee returns from Kenya, attributing the decision to a lack of available services and livelihoods for returnees.

Refugees and Somali returnees had limited access to basic services. Poor refugee reception services in Somaliland resulted in some refugees reportedly returning to Yemen despite continuing conflict.

Section 3. Freedom to Participate in the Political Process

The provisional constitution provides citizens the ability to choose their government in free and fair periodic elections, held by secret ballot and based on universal and equal suffrage, but citizens could not exercise that ability.

Elections and Political Participation

Recent Elections: In 2015 the FGS decided direct elections during the year would not be possible due to security concerns; it subsequently developed a plan for indirect elections by electoral colleges selected by elders. Indirect elections for the lower house of parliament, the new upper house, and the president, scheduled for August and September, had not been completed by year's end. Nevertheless, indirect elections for the lower house expanded the electorate from 135 elders to 14,025 electoral college delegates selected by the elders; 51 delegates selected by clan elders were responsible for voting on each lower house seat, and delegates were required to include 30 percent (16) women and 10 youths. Although 90 percent of the lower and upper house elections had concluded by year's end, elections for parliamentary leadership and a president had not begun. Allegations of vote-buying, intimidation, threats, interference by federal and regional officials, violence, and kidnapping were widespread ahead of voting.

In 2012 the TFG completed the 2011 Roadmap for Ending the Transition, collaborating with representatives of Puntland, Galmudug, the ASWJ, and the international community. The process included drafting a provisional federal constitution, forming an 825-member National Constituent Assembly (NCA) that ratified the provisional constitution, selecting a 275-member federal parliament, and holding speakership and presidential elections. The FGS was scheduled to review and amend the provisional constitution and submit it for approval in a national referendum by year's end, but the process was not completed.

Under the 2012 roadmap process, 135 traditional clan elders convened in Mogadishu to nominate 825 NCA delegates to consider the provisional federal constitution. The elders also nominated candidates for the country's 275-member federal parliament to serve four-year terms under the provisional constitution. There were accusations of bribery and intimidation involved in the selection of the 135 traditional elders and in their nomination of parliamentarians, but overall the roadmap signatories and others viewed parliamentarians as broadly representative of their communities.

In the presence of international observers, the parliament in 2012 held an indirect presidential election by secret ballot in which Hassan Sheikh Mohamud defeated incumbent TFG president Sheikh Sharif in the second and final round of voting. There were unsubstantiated reports of presidential candidates' bribing parliamentarians in exchange for their vote. Sheikh Sharif conceded defeat and described the vote as fair.

Somaliland laws prevent citizens in its region from participating in FGS-related processes.

In 2012 Puntland's constituent assembly overwhelmingly adopted a state constitution that enshrines a multiparty political system. In 2014 Abdiweli Mohamed Ali "Gaas" defeated incumbent President Abdirahman Mohamed Mohamed "Farole" by one parliamentary vote in a run-off election broadcast live on local television and radio stations. President Farole accepted the results. Parliament also elected Abdihakim Abdulahi as the new vice president.

The ISWA state parliament was formed in December 2015 following the 2014 state formation conference, which voted to elect Sharif Hassan Sheikh Adam as the interim region's first president.

In 2015 the FGS officially inaugurated the 89-member IGA assembly; the 89 members had been selected by 40 traditional elders representing 11 subclans. In July 2015 the assembly elected Abdikarim Hussein Guled as the IGA's first president. The ASWJ refused to accept the election results and unilaterally established its own self-declared administration for those parts of the IGA it controlled.

Parliamentary elections in Somaliland, last held in 2005, were overdue. Somaliland president Ahmed Mohamed Mohamud "Silanyo" was elected in 2010. International and domestic observers declared the election free and fair. Somaliland has a bicameral parliament consisting of an appointed 86-member House of Elders, known as the Guurti, and an elected 82-member House of Representatives with proportional clan representation. In April the House of Elders voted to postpone the delayed elections for the House of Representatives and president until March 2017. On September 10, however, Silanyo announced that parliamentary and presidential elections would be separated, prompting another delay of the parliamentary polls and another term extension. A new date for parliamentary elections had not been set by year's end. There were allegations the House of Elders was subject to political corruption and undue influence.

In 2013 the FGS and Jubaland delegates signed an agreement that resulted in the FGS's formal recognition of the newly formed IJA. Ahmed Mohamed Islam "Madobe" was selected as president in a 2013 conference of elders and representatives.

In January the FGS launched the state formation conference for Hiiraan and Middle Shabelle Regions, the final federal member state to be constituted within the federal system. The process concluded with the formation of Hirshabelle state in October, the formation of the Hirshabelle assembly on October 10, and the election of Hirshabelle president Ali Abdullahi Osoble on October 17. The state formation process was marred by allegations that the FGS president interfered with the process to influence the Somali presidential elections by placing his supporters in key positions in the new state administration and providing for significant representation by his subclan. The traditional leader of the Hawadle subclan, a large constituency in Hiiraan, refused to participate.

Al-Shabaab prohibited citizens in the areas it controlled from changing their al-Shabaab administrators. Some al-Shabaab administrations, however, consulted local traditional elders on specific issues and allowed preexisting district committees to remain in place.

<u>Political Parties and Political Participation</u>: In September the president signed the political parties law, which created the first framework for legal political parties since 1969, when former president Siad Barre banned political activities after

taking power in a coup. Prior to September, however, several political associations had operated as parties. For example, the FGS president claimed to be elected from the Peace and Development Party in 2012. The provisional constitution provides that every citizen has the right to take part in public affairs and that this right includes forming political parties, participating in their activities, and being elected for any position within a political party.

The Somaliland and Puntland constitutions and electoral legislation limit the number of political parties to three and established conditions pertaining to their political programs, finances, and constitutions.

On February 22, security forces arbitrarily arrested the deputy chairperson of the Banadiri Political Reformation Council following a public gathering of supporters in Mogadishu to advocate for Banadiri community rights. He was released after three days.

Participation of Women and Minorities: There are no laws limiting the participation of women in the political process, and women participated. Cultural factors, however, limited women's participation. While roadmap signatories agreed that women should hold at least 30 percent of the seats in the federal parliament prior to the country's transition to a permanent government, women held only 14 percent of 275 seats in parliament. Notwithstanding efforts to structure indirect elections to meet the 30 percent quota met significant resistance from clan elders, political leaders, and religious leaders, women's representation in parliament increased to 25 percent. The 26-member cabinet had only one woman after one female minister resigned during the year and a second was removed; both were replaced by men.

Civil society, minority clans, and Puntland authorities called for the abolition of the "4.5 formula" by which political representation was divided among the four major clans, with the minority clans combined as the remaining "0.5" share. This system allocated to minority clans a fixed and low number of slots in the federal parliament. Under the provisional constitution, the electoral process was intended to be direct and, thus, diverge from the 4.5 formula, but federal and regional leaders decided in April to revert to the 4.5 formula in determining lower house composition. Former prime minister Abdiweli and Prime Minister Sharmarke maintained the same ratio of minority representation when expanding the cabinet until June, when two of the three female ministers were replaced with men.

Somaliland had two women in its 86-member House of Representatives. The sole woman occupying a seat in the House of Elders gained appointment after her husband, who occupied the seat, resigned in 2012. Women traditionally were excluded from the House of Elders. There were two female ministers among the 24 cabinet ministers.

A woman chaired the Somaliland Human Rights Commission, while a minority youth served as deputy chair. The Somaliland president kept a presidential advisor on minority problems. In August, President Silanyo appointed a member of the Dhulbahante, a politically marginalized subclan within Somaliland, to lead the Interior Ministry, which is responsible for complaints of marginalization by minority communities in the Sool and Sanaag contested regions.

Women have never served on the Council of Elders in Puntland. Traditional clan elders, all men, selected members of Puntland's House of Representatives. Two women served in the 66-member House of Representatives. The minister of women and family affairs and the minster of constitution, federalism, and democratization were women. The nine-member electoral commission included one woman.

Section 4. Corruption and Lack of Transparency in Government

Government officials frequently engaged in corrupt practices. The law provides for criminal penalties for corruption by officials, but the government did not implement the law effectively. In October 2015 the SEMG noted the "apparent impunity enjoyed by those who have engaged in misappropriation of public finances perpetuates a culture of corruption in Somali politics."

Corruption: In May government officials claimed a government-staffed internal review of the 2015 Soma Oil and Gas Company deal found no wrongdoing. A 2015 SEMG annex report documented that Soma paid more than half million dollars (equivalent to 286 billion Somalia shillings) to senior civil servants in the Ministry of Petroleum and Mineral Resources under the rubric of "capacity building agreement." According to the report, several ministry officials received salaries simultaneously from the FGS and Soma Oil and Gas. The government did not release the review, and none of the employees that received salaries from Soma or the government were dismissed.

The Financial Governance Committee (FGC)--an advisory body with no legal authority but responsible for reviewing all government contracts for more than 2.8 billion Somalia shillings (five million dollars)--consisted of six FGS members and four delegates funded by international financial institutions. Although compliance among government ministries, departments, and agencies continued to improve, some ministries bypassed the FGC when negotiating important public contracts.

The SEMG continued to report on the export of charcoal in violation of a UN Security Council ban. Charcoal production and export continued in areas controlled by al-Shabaab, the IJA, and Kenyan AMISOM forces; most of the illegal export was from Kismayo, according to the SEMG.

Somaliland had a national auditor and a governance and anticorruption commission appointed by Somaliland's president. Somaliland did not try any Somaliland officials for corruption.

Puntland's Good Governance and Anticorruption Commission did not investigate any Puntland officials for corruption.

Al-Shabaab extorted high and unpredictable "zakat" (a Muslim obligation to donate to charity during Ramadan) and "sadaqa" (a voluntary charity contribution paid by Muslims) taxes in the regions it controlled. Al-Shabaab also diverted and stole humanitarian food aid.

Financial Disclosure: The law does not require income and asset disclosure by appointed or elected officials.

Public Access to Information: The provisional constitution states that citizens have the right of access to information held by the state. It also states that parliament shall enact a law to provide for this right, but parliament had not approved such a law by year's end.

Section 5. Governmental Attitude Regarding International and Nongovernmental Investigation of Alleged Violations of Human Rights

A number of local and international human rights groups operated in areas outside al-Shabaab-controlled territory, investigating and publishing their findings on human rights cases. Government officials were somewhat cooperative and responsive to their views, although they also harassed NGOs. Security concerns constrained NGOs' ability to operate in southern and central areas. On June 8, for example, unknown gunmen in Galkayo town shot and killed the head of an NGO (see section 1.a.). International and local NGOs generally worked without major restrictions in Puntland and Somaliland.

Authorities sometimes harassed or did not cooperate with NGOs. For example, in matters related to official corruption, the government regularly dismissed the findings of international and local NGOs as well as of internal auditors.

Government Human Rights Bodies: The provisional federal constitution calls for the formation of an independent national human rights commission and a truth and reconciliation commission within 45 days and 30 days, respectively, of the formation of the Council of Ministers in 2012. On August 14, the FGS president signed the human rights commission bill into law, although commissioners had not been appointed by year's end. No action on the proposed truth and reconciliation commission had been taken by year's end.

Limited resources as well as inexperienced commissioners restricted the effectiveness of the Somaliland Human Rights Commission and Puntland's Human Rights Defender Office.

Section 6. Discrimination, Societal Abuses, and Trafficking in Persons

Women

Rape and Domestic Violence: The law criminalizes rape, providing penalties of five to 15 years in prison for violations. Military court sentences for rape included death. The government did not effectively enforce the law. There are no laws against spousal violence, including rape, although on May 27, the Council of Ministers approved a national gender policy that gives the state the right to sue anyone convicted of committing gender-based violence, such as the killing or rape of a woman. Somali NGOs documented patterns of rape perpetrated with impunity, particularly of female IDPs and members of minority clans.

Although statistics on cases of gender-based violence in Mogadishu were unreliable, international and local NGOs characterized such violence as pervasive. Government forces, militia members, and men wearing uniforms raped women and girls. While the army arrested some security force members accused of such rapes, impunity was the norm.

AMISOM troops committed sexual abuse and exploitation, including rape.

Women feared reporting rape due to possible reprisals. Police were reluctant to investigate and sometimes asked survivors to do the investigatory work for their own cases. Traditional approaches to dealing with rape tended to ignore the survivor's situation and instead sought resolution or compensation for rape through a negotiation between clan members of the perpetrator and survivor. Some survivors were forced to marry perpetrators.

For the most part, authorities rarely used formal structures to address rape. Survivors suffered from subsequent discrimination based on the attribution of "impurity."

Local civil society organizations in Somaliland reported that gang rape continued to be a problem in urban areas, primarily perpetrated by youth gangs and male students. It often occurred in poorer neighborhoods and among immigrants, returned refugees, and displaced rural populations living in urban areas. In 55 percent of reported cases, a minor was the victim. Many cases went unreported.

Domestic and sexual violence against women remained serious problems despite the provisional federal constitution provision prohibiting any form of violence against women. While both sharia and customary law address the resolution of family disputes, women were not included in the decision-making process.

Al-Shabaab also committed sexual violence, including through forced marriages. Al-Shabaab sentenced persons to death for rape.

Female Genital Mutilation/Cutting (FGM/C): Although the provisional federal constitution describes female circumcision as cruel and degrading, equates it with torture, and prohibits the circumcision of girls, FGM/C was almost universally practiced throughout the country. UNICEF reported that 98 percent of women and girls had undergone FGM/C and that the majority were subjected to infibulation-- the most severe form--which involves cutting and sewing the genitalia. At least 80 percent of Somali girls who have undergone FGM/C had the procedure performed when they were between the ages of five and 14. International and local NGOs conducted education awareness programs on the dangers of FGM/C, but there were no reliable statistics to measure their success. In March the prime minister expressed support for an international campaign, led by activist group Avaaz, to encourage the country to adopt a zero tolerance approach to FGM/C. The campaign collected more than 1.3 million signatures.

Other Harmful Traditional Practices: Adultery in al-Shabaab-controlled areas was punishable by death; unlike in prior years, there were no reports of women being stoned to death for adultery.

<u>Sexual Harassment</u>: The provisional federal constitution states that workers, particularly women, shall have a special right of protection from sexual abuse and discrimination. Nevertheless, sexual harassment was believed to be widespread. No information was available on governmental programs addressing sexual harassment.

<u>Reproductive Rights</u>: A woman's husband often made decisions regarding the couple's reproduction. Women had little ability to decide freely and responsibly the number, spacing, and timing of their children or manage their reproductive health. They also had limited information about contraception or access to it. According to the United Nations, an estimated 15 percent of girls and women between the ages of 15 and 49 used some form of contraception. Women rarely had skilled attendants during pregnancy and childbirth, emergency care for complications arising from abortion, or essential obstetric and postpartum care.

The United Nations reported that more than 80 percent of internally displaced women had no access to safe maternal delivery. The maternal mortality ratio was 732 per 100,000 live births due to complications during labor that often involved anemia, FGM/C, and the lack of medical care. This represented an improvement since 2010, when the ratio was 850 per 100,000 live births. A woman's lifetime risk of maternal death was one in 18.

<u>Discrimination</u>: Women did not have the same rights as men and experienced systematic subordination to men, despite provisions in the federal constitution prohibiting such discrimination. Women experienced discrimination in credit, education, politics, and housing.

On May 27, the Council of Ministers approved a national gender policy plan to increase women's political participation, economic empowerment, and the education of girls. The plan included programs to promote awareness and sensitivity to gender issues and tools to measure gender inequities in policies and programs. On June 30, the Somali Islamic Scholars Union denounced the new policy as un-Islamic and called for punishment of its authors. In June and July, the minister of women, human rights, and social development, the only woman remaining in the cabinet, reportedly received several death threats from extremist Islamic groups who accused her of pushing for women's representation in government. On October 2, the Somali Religious Council released a press statement warning the government against advocating for women in politics, calling the 30 percent quota for women's seats in parliament "dangerous" and against Islamic religious tenets and predicting the policy would lead to disintegration of the family.

Only men administered sharia, which often was applied in the interests of men. According to sharia law and the local tradition of blood compensation, anyone found guilty of the death of a woman paid to the victim's family only half the amount required to compensate for a man's death.

While the law requires equal pay for equal work, this did not always occur. Women were underrepresented in both the formal public and private sectors because of cultural norms and girls' low educational level. Women were not subject to discrimination in owning or managing businesses except in al-Shabaab-controlled areas. While generally visible in micro- and small enterprises, women were relegated to lower-level positions in larger companies.

The exclusion of women was more pronounced in al-Shabaab-controlled areas, where women's participation in economic activities was perceived as anti-Islamic.

While formal law and sharia provide women the right to own and dispose of property independently, various legal, cultural, and societal barriers often obstructed women from exercising such rights. By law girls and women could inherit only half the amount of property to which their brothers were entitled. A 2010 report from a local women's organization in Somaliland indicated 75 percent of women did not own livestock, land, or other property. Only 15 to 20 percent received inheritance from male family members.

Children

Birth Registration: The provisional federal constitution provides that there is only one Somali citizenship and calls for a special law defining how to obtain, suspend, or lose it. As of year's end, parliament had not passed such a law.

According to UNICEF data from 2005 to 2012, authorities registered 3 percent of births in the country. Authorities in Puntland and in the southern and central regions did not register births. Birth registration occurred in Somaliland for hospital and home births, but limited capacity combined with the nomadic lifestyle of many persons caused numerous births in the region to go unregistered. In 2014 UNICEF began to support the Somaliland government in establishing a birth registration system by district. According to the most recent statistics, the system had registered 5,300 births by November 2015; the program aimed to register approximately 270,000 children. Failure to register births did not result in denial of public services, such as education.

Education: The provisional constitution provides the right to a free education up to the secondary level, but education was not free, compulsory, or universal. Education needs were partially met by a patchwork of institutions, including a traditional system of Quranic schools; public primary and secondary school systems financed by communities, foreign donors, and the Somaliland and Puntland administrations; Islamic charity-run schools; and a number of privately run primary and secondary schools and vocational training institutes. In many areas, children did not have access to schools other than madrassas. Attendance rates for girls remained lower than for boys.

Child Abuse: Child abuse and rape of children were serious problems, although no statistics on their prevalence were available. There were no known efforts by the government or regional governments to combat child abuse. Children remained among the chief victims of continuing societal violence.

The practice of "asi walid," whereby parents placed their children in boarding schools, other institutions, and sometimes prison for disciplinary purposes and without any legal procedure, allegedly continued throughout the country.

Early and Forced Marriage: The provisional federal constitution requires both marriage partners to have reached the "age of maturity" and defines a child as a person less than 18 years old. It notes marriage requires the free consent of both the man and woman to be legal. Early marriages frequently occurred; 45 percent of women between the ages of 20 and 24 were married by age 18 and 8 percent were married by the age of 15. In rural areas, parents often compelled daughters as young as 12 to marry. In areas under its control, al-Shabaab arranged compulsory marriages between its soldiers and young girls and used the lure of marriage as a recruitment tool. There were no known efforts by the government or regional authorities to prevent early and forced marriage.

Female Genital Mutilation/Cutting (FGM/C): See information on girls under 18 in the women's section above.

Sexual Exploitation of Children: Child prostitution is illegal in all regions. There is no statutory rape law or minimum age for consensual sex. The law does not expressly prohibit child pornography. The law on sexual exploitation was rarely enforced, and such exploitation reportedly was frequent.

<u>Child Soldiers</u>: The use of child soldiers remained a problem (see section 1.g.).

<u>Displaced Children</u>: There was a large population of IDPs and children who lived and worked on the streets.

<u>International Child Abductions</u>: The country is not a party to the 1980 Hague Convention on the Civil Aspects of International Child Abduction. See the Department of State's *Annual Report on International Parental Child Abduction* at <u>travel.state.gov/content/childabduction/en/legal/compliance.html</u>.

Anti-Semitism

There was no known Jewish community, and there were no reports of anti-Semitic acts.

Trafficking in Persons

See the Department of State's *Trafficking in Persons Report* at <u>www.state.gov/j/tip/rls/tiprpt/</u>.

Persons with Disabilities

The provisional federal constitution provides equal rights before the law for persons with disabilities and prohibits the state from discriminating against them. Authorities did not enforce these provisions. The provisional federal constitution does not specify whether this provision applies to physical, intellectual, mental, or sensory disabilities. It does not discuss discrimination by nongovernmental actors, including with regard to employment, education, air travel and other transportation, or provision of health care. The law does not mandate access to buildings, information, or communications for persons with disabilities.

The needs of most persons with disabilities were not addressed. A report by the World Health Organization and Swedish International Development Aid (SIDA) estimated that up to 15 percent of the population was physically disabled. In 2011 SIDA found that 25 percent of public buildings were designed for wheelchair accessibility but no public transportation facilities had wheelchair access.

According to Amnesty International, persons with disabilities faced daily human rights abuses, such as unlawful killings, violence including rape and other forms of sexual violence, forced evictions, and lack of access to health care or an adequate standard of living. Domestic violence and forced marriage were prevalent practices affecting persons with disabilities. Women and girls with disabilities faced an increased risk of rape and other forms of sexual violence, often with impunity, due to perceptions their disabilities were a burden to the family or that such persons were of less value and could be abused.

Several local NGOs in Somaliland provided services for persons with disabilities and reported numerous cases of discrimination and abuse. These NGOs reported that persons with mental and physical disabilities faced widespread discrimination and that it was common and condoned by the community for students without disabilities to beat and harass those with disabilities.

Without a public health infrastructure, few services existed to provide support or education for persons with mental disabilities. It was common for such persons to be chained to a tree or restrained within their homes.

Local organizations advocated for the rights of persons with disabilities with negligible support from local authorities.

National/Racial/Ethnic Minorities

More than 85 percent of the population shared a common ethnic heritage, religion, and nomad-influenced culture. In most areas, the predominant clan excluded members of other groups from effective participation in governing institutions and subjected them to discrimination in employment, judicial proceedings, and access to public services.

Minority groups included the Bantu (the largest minority group), Banadiri, Reer Hamar, Brawanese, Swahili, Tumal, Yibir, Yaxar, Madhiban, Hawrarsame, Muse Dheryo, Faqayaqub, and Gabooye. Minority groups, often lacking armed militias, continued to be disproportionately subjected to killings, torture, rape, kidnapping for ransom, and looting of land and property with impunity by faction militias and majority clan members, often with the acquiescence of federal and local authorities. Many minority communities continued to live in deep poverty and to suffer from numerous forms of discrimination and exclusion.

Representatives of minority clans in the federal parliament were targeted by unknown assailants, whom minority clan members alleged were paid by majority clan members. Somali returnees and IDPs from minority clans suffered discrimination, since they often lacked powerful clan connections and protection.

Fighting between clans resulted in deaths and injuries. For example, in Hiiraan 16 civilians were killed and 28 injured in recurrent clan fighting between the Gaaljecel and Jajeele in Beledweyne and rural villages in the area. On September 5, at least 15 persons were killed and 40 injured in clan fighting between the Sacad subclan of the Hawiye and the Omar Mahmoud subclan of the Darood in rural areas east of Galkayo town in Mudug Region. In Lower Shabelle Region, fighting between Habargidir and Biyomaal subclans resulted in 28 civilian deaths during the year.

Deaths from the July 2015 conflict between Dhulbahante and Habar Yunis clans in Guumeys village, Somaliland, were settled during the year by the transfer of blood money.

Acts of Violence, Discrimination, and Other Abuses Based on Sexual Orientation and Gender Identity

Same-sex sexual contact is punishable by imprisonment for two months to three years. The law does not prohibit discrimination based on sexual orientation or gender identity. Society considered sexual orientation and gender identity taboo topics, and there was no known public discussion of discrimination based on sexual orientation or gender identity in any region. There were no known LGBTI organizations and no reports of events. There were few reports of societal violence or discrimination based on sexual orientation or gender identity due to severe societal stigma that prevented LGBTI individuals from making their sexual orientation or gender identity known publicly. There were no known actions to investigate or punish those complicit in abuses. Hate crime laws or other criminal justice mechanisms did not exist to aid in the prosecution of bias-motivated crimes against members of the LGBTI community.

HIV and AIDS Social Stigma

Persons with HIV/AIDS continued to face discrimination and abuse in their local communities and by employers in all regions. The United Nations reported that persons with HIV/AIDS experienced physical abuse, rejection by their families, and workplace discrimination and dismissal. Children of HIV-positive parents also suffered discrimination, which hindered access to services. There was no official response to such discrimination.

Section 7. Worker Rights

a. Freedom of Association and the Right to Collective Bargaining

The provisional federal constitution provides for the right of every worker to form and join a trade union, to participate in the activities of a trade union, to conduct legal strikes, and to engage in collective bargaining. No specific legal restrictions existed that limited these rights. The law does not provide limits on the scope of collective bargaining. The provisional federal constitution does not address antiunion discrimination or the reinstatement of workers fired for union activity. Legal protections did not exclude any particular groups of workers. While penalties included six months in jail, which would likely serve as a sufficient deterrent, the government lacked the capacity to enforce applicable laws effectively.

In November the International Labor Organization's (ILO's) Committee on Freedom of Association upheld a 2015 complaint filed by two Somali trade unions and supported by the International Trade Union Confederation. The ILO urged the government to refrain from any further interference in the unions. The complaints concerned violations of the Right to Organize and Collective Bargaining Convention and the Freedom of Association and Protection of the Right to Organize Convention. The complaint detailed systematic violations of freedom of association and trade union rights by the government, including undermining the independence and legitimacy of the trade union movement and harassment and intimidation of union members and leaders by government agencies. The complaint also noted that the country's labor legislation was outdated and clearly inadequate to protect trade union rights.

Government and employers did not respect freedom of association. The government repeatedly interfered in union activities. For example, the government unilaterally revoked approval of the Federation of Somali Trade Unions' delegation to the June 2015 International Labor Conference.

b. Prohibition of Forced or Compulsory Labor

The provisional federal constitution prohibits slavery, servitude, trafficking, or forced labor for any purpose. Authorities did not effectively enforce the law. Under the pre-1991 penal code, applicable at the federal and regional levels, the penalty for slavery is imprisonment for five to 20 years. The penalty for using forced labor is imprisonment for six months to five years. Although the penalties appeared sufficiently stringent, they were rarely enforced. There were no known efforts by the government to prevent or eliminate forced labor in the country. The Ministry of Labor did not have an inspectorate and did not conduct any labor-related inspections.

Forced labor occurred. Children and minority clan members were reportedly used as porters to transport the mild narcotic khat (or "miraa"); in farming and animal herding; in crushing stones; and in construction. Al-Shabaab forced persons in their camps to move to the countryside, reportedly to raise cash crops for the organization.

Also see the Department of State's *Trafficking in Persons Report* at www.state.gov/j/tip/rls/tiprpt/.

c. Prohibition of Child Labor and Minimum Age for Employment

It was unclear whether there was a minimum age for employment. The pre-1991 labor code prohibits child labor, provides a legal minimum age of 15 for most employment, prescribes different minimum ages for certain hazardous activities, and prohibits those under 18 from night work in the industrial, commercial, and agricultural sectors, apart from work that engages family members only. The provisional federal constitution states, "No child may perform work or provide services that are not suitable for the child's age or create a risk to the child's health or development in any way." The provisional federal constitution defines a child as any person less than 18 years old.

The federal Ministries of Labor and of Women and Human Rights Development are responsible for enforcing child labor laws. The ministries, however, did not enforce these laws. Many of the laws related to the commercial exploitation of children are included in the 1962 penal code. These laws were not adequate to prevent child labor, as many of the fines were negligible due to inflation. The government participated in campaigns to remove children from participation in armed conflict (see section 1.g.).

Child labor was widespread. The recruitment and use of child soldiers remained a problem (see section 1.g.). Youths commonly worked in herding, agriculture, and household labor from an early age. Children broke rocks into gravel and worked as vendors of cigarettes and khat on the streets. UNICEF estimated that 49 percent of children between ages five and 14 were in the workforce between 2009 and 2015.

Also see the Department of Labor's *Findings on the Worst Forms of Child Labor* at www.dol.gov/ilab/reports/child-labor/findings/.

d. Discrimination with Respect to Employment and Occupation

The law and regulations prohibit discrimination regarding race, sex, disability, political opinion, color, language, or social status, but the government did not effectively enforce those laws and regulations. The labor code requires equal pay for equal work. According to the 1972 labor code, penalties included imprisonment up to six months and/or a fine of not more than 1,000 Somalia shillings (less than two dollars). Penalties were not sufficient to deter violations. The law does not prohibit discrimination on the basis of religion, age, national origin, social origin, sexual orientation or gender identity, or HIV-positive status or other communicable diseases.

e. Acceptable Conditions of Work

There was no national minimum wage. According to the World Bank, 52 percent of the population covered by the Somali High Frequency Survey Wave One lived in poverty.

The labor code provides for a standard workweek of 48 hours and at least nine paid national holidays and 15 days' annual leave, requires premium pay for overtime, and limits overtime to a maximum of 12 hours per week. The law sets occupational health and safety standards. The law does not specifically address whether workers can remove themselves from situations that endanger health or safety without jeopardy to their employment.

There was no organized effort to monitor working conditions. The Ministry of Labor was responsible at the federal level for enforcement, although it was not effective.

Wages and working conditions were established largely through arrangements based on supply, demand, and the influence of workers' clans. There was no information on the existence or status of foreign or migrant workers in the country. Most workers worked in the informal sector.

Authorities did not have the capacity to protect workers who wished to remove themselves from situations that endangered their health or safety, although no such cases were reported.

www.ingramcontent.com/pod-product-compliance
Lightning Source LLC
Chambersburg PA
CBHW081253250726
48654CB00012B/1597